P.S.

Passionate Supporter and Political Spouse

ANDREA WHITE

ISBN 978-0-615-28359-3

LCCN 2009902456

Printed in the United States of America

First Edition

To order additional copies of *P.S.*, visit www.andreawhiteauthor.com
or visit her blog at www.passionatesupporter.com.

Yao's big night propels Rockets past Pistons / **Sports**

Houston Chronicle

www.HoustonChronicle.com | SUNDAY, DECEMBER 7, 2003

It's White in a landslide

Green ousts Keller; Sekula-Gibbs wins

By KRISTEN MACK
Houston Chronicle

CEO captures mayor's office

By JOHN WILLIAMS
Houston Chronicle Political Writer

WHITE, 62%   SANCHEZ, 38%

Mayor-elect Bill White shakes hands with supporters after Saturday's runoff.

See COUNCIL on Page 21A

See MAYOR on Page 30A

SPORTS

No. 1 Sooners
fall 35-7 to
Kansas State
Page 1B

Passionate Support

My husband, Bill White, served as mayor of Houston from 2004 through 2009. When Bill first told our three kids that he had decided he wanted to run for mayor, their responses reflected their personalities.

Our oldest, Will, who was in high school at the time, said, "Please, Dad, don't. You'll embarrass us."

Elena, our only daughter, said, "If you think you can make the city a better place, you should do it."

Stephen, our youngest, asked, "When can I be on television?"

My response was more complicated, and it changed greatly from beginning to end. I started out a reluctant Political Spouse. However, as I watched Bill getting so much accomplished and changing things in Houston, I got caught up in the excitement of hoping and believing that government can be better.

What took me so long? Why had I spent so much time on the sidelines? Because I was scared I would fail? Because I didn't dare to believe?

All I know is that when I truly got into my role as Political Spouse and became a Passionate Supporter of Bill's, a whole new world opened up to me. And I am now passionate about it.

When you care about something larger than yourself, you end up growing. This whole political experience has pulled me out of myself. It's not only that I'm there for Bill more: I'm there for my kids more; I'm there for my friends more; I'm there for myself more.

I've become the kind of person who can be a Passionate Supporter because I'm not as scared as I once was. I recognize that my time on this earth is limited and I want to have my impact. I still Pause and Stumble sometimes. But it's exciting to be growing.

BEST P.S. MOMENT EVER

One night about halfway through Bill's third term,
he came home, sat down at the dinner table, and said,
"I love my job."

Our family

Plain and Simple

I love my job, too. So much that I wanted to share my journey from Plain and Simple Political Spouse to Passionate Supporter. What follows are journal entries I jotted down during my time as Political Spouse. Looking back on them, I recognized the P.S. theme that seems to have become a part of my life.

Public Speaking. I feared it.

Personal Stories. Here are mine. I'd like to know yours.

Political Savvy. I don't have it.

Public Servant. Bill's one of the best.

Passionate Supporter. What I've become.

And in a Politically Serious world, it's important to have a little fun.

2003

POLITICS SOMEDAY?

PRECIOUS SUPPORT

PRACTICAL SHOES

PERSONAL SCENARIOS

PLEASANT (AND UNPLEASANT)
SURPRISES

PRETTY STICKY

POSSIBLY SO AND SO???

Our first date: a canoe trip on the Neches

January 2003

Politics Someday?

Bill has never been one to sit on the sidelines. I knew that from the day I met him. I've always been more of a spectator. I didn't really want him to run for public office. I was scared. On the other hand, I didn't want to stand in his way. I gave him my blessing and kept my deep reservations to myself.

Bill and I met in law school, though we didn't know each other well. Later, we reconnected as friends. According to Bill, I proposed to him after our second date. My memory is different. But somehow after a ski trip, both of us agree, things grew serious.

Bill had always been interested in politics. In fact, he had almost run for office before we got married. But, when we were dating, we never once discussed it. Politics had seemed like only a remote possibility during our seventeen years of marriage. Far off in the distance. Someday. Maybe. Probably not. Until the year before he decided to run for mayor.

When the decision is made, the implications hit you like a truck.

Even if I had known from day one that Bill was going to run, I don't know how I could have prepared for the role of Political Spouse. How to get ready to judge dog shows? How to build up my endurance for four events in one night? How to develop thick skin?

I'm just grateful to have had a chance to learn as I go.

A TYPICAL PARTICULARLY STRESSFUL DAY

During the campaign, Pam, Bill's secretary, called to say that he was going to stop by the house for a quick dinner and jog before a televised debate.

She called back to say that he would run in for a quick dinner only. Within minutes, she called to say he was going directly to the station and would eat a couple of energy bars in the car.

When he finally got home late that night, I asked him, "Are you hungry or did the energy bars fill you up?"

He looked at me perplexed. "What energy bars?"

April 2003

Precious Support

Pretend a mountain has appeared in your backyard
overnight. In the morning, you know you must clear
it. With a heavy heart, you and your spouse grab
shovels. When you go outside, you see that a crowd of
people are busy...digging. This is what a campaign
feels like.

    People supported Bill in droves. It was a
wonderful mix of friends I would expect and those I
never would have guessed, along with many I didn't
know. Our campaign office became a busy hub filled
with volunteers of different backgrounds and
ethnicities. On one end of the spectrum, we had
seniors who worked hard and appreciated the meals
and the company. Then we had teenagers, some
fulfilling high school civic requirements and

others simply enthusiastic about the process of government. The office hummed with positive energy and interesting conversations.

We are people who don't like to ask for favors, but after a while, I conquered my discomfort about asking for help. Not the asking for money part; I am still reluctant to do that. But as the campaign unfolded, the cause just sort of took over. I began to overcome my self-consciousness and understand that the effort wasn't about me, or even Bill. I started to feel like, "I'm not asking for help for my husband. I'm asking people to participate in good government."

Once I made that transition, I outgrew my embarrassment and relaxed.

FUNNIEST P.S. MOMENT

A woman in her late 50's or early 60's came up to me at a reception for city employees. Bill had just eliminated Viagra reimbursement from the city's health policy, saving the city over $800,000 a year.

She said, "Are you Bill White's wife?"

I told her, "Yes."

She said, "I really want to thank you. Your husband is the greatest mayor ever. I was getting tired; my man…it's unnatural. Your husband's going to be mayor for a long time, right?"

A few minutes later, I saw her walking out with an elderly man leaning on a cane.

Oh my!

May 2003

Practical Shoes

There is an old saying that I believe holds true: "You are only as happy as your unhappiest child." And I think it's also true that you're only as happy as your unhappiest foot.

I really admire all the fashionable shoes I see at events, but I can't help feeling a little sorry for those squashed toes, those aching arches.

Give me a choice between fashion or comfort, and I'll choose comfort every time.

Since I love to exercise, my favorite shoes are tennis shoes. Maybe that's why my only question to Bill when he first mentioned running for office was, "Do I have to dress up all the time?"

He answered, "No."

That was a relief.

Shortly after Bill was elected, a friend of mine told me that she had actually negotiated a contract with her husband before he ran for office. Her pre-nuptial-style political agreement listed all the things she didn't want to do.

I wasn't that smart; I had no idea that a spouse could contract for her level of participation. But looking back on that early conversation with Bill, I understand now that it was a negotiation of sorts. And I'm glad I have a tennis shoes clause in my contract.

BECOMING A POLITICAL SPOUSE CAN FEEL LIKE DONNING A NEW HAT

At official functions, some people can see only the hat. The peacock feathers and the sequins sticking out distract them, and they ask, "What should I call you now? Your Honor?" They mock bow when they see you. Some people understand that you know that the hat comes off. You have less time for yourself, but otherwise you are the same.

June 2003

Personal Scenarios

As the hurly-burly of a campaign grinds on, your regular life still demands attention. Sometimes, you can feel pulled in a thousand directions, but thank goodness for carpools, dinners, and doctor appointments. These details keep you grounded and remind you that no matter what happens, your real life waits for you.

Every day, I would watch Bill get up at 6 a.m. and head out the door, only to return at 9 or 10 p.m., or later. Every day, I would ask myself, "Do I need to give up what I love? Am I a slacker if I don't devote myself single-mindedly to the campaign?"

I'm not sure when I reached my decision. It certainly wasn't a formal one.

Sure, I worked hard. But even though the campaign cut deeply into Bill's most cherished time, reading, bicycling, enjoying our kids and our friends, I decided to preserve the parts of my life that I loved. I kept a somewhat regular family life, kept writing and exercising. I didn't tell anybody—and until now, I haven't advertised it. But that was my decision. And guess what? I don't resent the time I spent campaigning.

PHENOMENAL SCRIBE

I began writing for teens when I was forty and had my first book published after Bill took office. In that book, Surviving Antarctica, *I gave each of my five characters a special gift like a photographic memory, an ability to withstand the cold, and a gamer's instinct. But I found myself sadly lacking.*

During the campaign, my mother and I (mostly my mother) wrote thank-you notes to donors. I found I could write fifty notes at one sitting. At the same time, Surviving Antarctica *was published and I signed hundreds of books.*

People would always ask, "Isn't your wrist tired?" I kept answering, "No," until I finally realized I did have a special gift—an iron wrist.

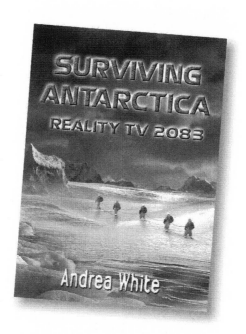

My first book

August 2003

Pretty Sticky

A campaign affects all aspects of your life: your diet (too much fast food); your social life (you don't have much of one), and your car (its bumper). I had never put a bumper sticker on my car until Bill ran for mayor. Prior to that, I felt whom I voted for was a private matter.

I don't know if all voters who are passionate about their candidates feel this way, but driving around with a "Bill White for Mayor" bumper sticker made me a particularly courteous driver. I don't think I'm a bad driver, but with that tag on my car, I tried to be an excellent driver.

I doubt anyone ever said or thought anything along these lines, but I imagined many a driver in a car passing me, leaning over, and commenting on my driving: "Those Bill White for Mayor folks are such nice drivers." It was the most indirect get-out-the-vote effort ever launched. Unfortunately, I have to admit that my sixteen-year-old teenager, who also had a Bill White bumper sticker on his car, probably lost every hypothetical vote that I won.

Which brings me to my point here: convince your candidate to use magnetic bumper stickers.

The day after Bill won, I tried to peel my bumper sticker off with soap and water. Those things are hard to remove!

A PLUNGE IN THE SWIMMING POOL

Sometimes you just have to jump in. After a lap, I am no longer cold and feel wonderful. Once I actually walk through the door of a political event, I'm glad I'm there. But when I'm pulling on my swimsuit or applying my lipstick, I'm filled with doubts. It's the transitions that are hard.

September 2003

Possibly So and So???

You are exposed to thousands of names during a campaign. If I occasionally have trouble retrieving words, I have an even harder time with names. Of course, half the time when you're introduced to someone, you never really even hear the name—which makes your task impossible from the start.

Then, nine times out of ten, you hear the name and that's all you ever learn about the person. I have a much better chance of remembering someone's name if I also have an interesting fact to hang onto, such as Salina enjoys fishing off South Padre Island or Dale's daughter is into stamp collecting.

What happens when you are introduced to people and you actually have a brief conversation? Now you have a reason to remember them—but how do you do it?

I have tried a number of mnemonic devices, but haven't found one that works. If the petite woman with black hair standing before me says her name is Wendy and I can't think of anything else, I might associate her with Peter Pan. The next time I meet the petite woman, I'll repeat, Peter Pan, Peter Pan. She's small, could she be Tinker Bell? So is her name Belle? Or did I remember Peter Pan because her name is Pam?

When my stratagems fail, I blab on and on, and sometimes a tiny miracle occurs. The name, which has been playing an annoying game of hide-and-seek with my mind, gets tired of waiting and just pops out of my mouth.

I guess my policy has become try, try, try, and then forgive, forgive, forgive.

IT'S HARD TO GET A PERFECT SCORE IN THE NAME GAME

You call Jane "Harriet" every single time you meet.

MINUS 20.

You remember an unusual name like Glorishaba or Alicianora.

10 BONUS POINTS.

You actually forget a good friend's name.

MINUS 150.

You mumble the name and hope the person doesn't notice.

MINUS 10.

You can see their nametag and actually read it before the person notices.

5 BONUS POINTS.

2004

PROPER, BUT STUFFY

POWERFUL SERIES

YOU KNOW YOU'RE A
POLITICAL SPOUSE WHEN...

POINTLESS SESSIONS

PUBLIC SPEAKING

POTENTIAL SPEED BUMPS

PREPARE FOR SNAFUS

PLAN SKILLFULLY

PRECIOUS SECONDS

PERSUADING STUDENTS

January 2004

Proper, but Stuffy

Who came up with the term "First Lady?" I wanted to know.

"First Lady" has its origins in the chiefly British term "Lady," a general title of nobility used to address the wife, widow, and sometimes daughter or daughter-in-law of a Knight, Viscount, Duke, Earl, and other titled men.

"First Lady" has also been reported to be an English translation of the Italian term "Prima Donna," the title given to the feminine lead in an opera.

My research confirmed my suspicion. "First Lady" sounds as if you're better than other people.

As girls, we were taught never to stand out or hold ourselves above anyone else. As early as kindergarten, you were scorned and isolated if you did. So the title "First Lady" goes against the grain.

Often at events, an organizer will announce, "The First Lady of Houston is with us," and I'm called upon to stand and wave. While I believe the title is necessary in some circumstances, I cringe inwardly at the term.

But this aristocratic title has lingered in the midst of our democratic culture for a reason. No one can think of a better alternative. I spent an afternoon in a dentist's chair trying to come up with a short, unisex term of respect that wasn't self-important. All the names I came up with were ridiculous—Elected Spousal Partner (ESP!), Spousal Unit, The Other One, Supreme Volunteer.

When people ask what they should call me, I can answer that. I say, "Call me Andrea."

P.S. TIP

At the beginning of Bill's term, a group of friends gave me some good advice. "Pick a focus and use it to screen requests or you'll be pulled in too many directions." Whether you are trying to shape the next few days or years, it really helps to have a clear priority.

January 2004

Powerful Series

There's no road map or guidebook for a Political Spouse, just plenty of expectations, many of them conflicting. You can have real power and responsibility or just smile a lot. Work sixty hours a week at the job or none. You can make this unique volunteer job into whatever you want it to be.

The role I charted for myself fell somewhere in between. I didn't want Bill's term to end with my wishing that I had seen more places in the city and met more people. I won't have those regrets, in large part because of a program that we started called We're All Neighbors. Each month, We're All Neighbors hosts a different program with a new group at an untried venue.

We're All Neighbors has celebrated the Persian New Year with a Farsi poet-turned-real-estate-

broker and enjoyed St. Patrick's Day tea with retiring
nuns from the Sisters of Charity of Incarnate Word.
We've visited the Art Car Museum, home of the first
and largest art car parade in the world; had dinner
with the women of the Houston Police and Fire
Department; attended an exhibit at the Museum of
Fine Arts, Houston, featuring African artists during
Black History Month; learned about Islam and the
modern Muslim woman at the Ishmaeli Center; and
visited Vision Beyond Boundaries, where a remark-
able student recited his moving poem in rap style.

Next month, we're going bird-watching. I
can't wait.

P.S. TIP

Eleanor Roosevelt was Pithy and Succinct in her advice about campaign behavior. She said, "Always be on time. Do as little talking as humanly possible. Lean back in the parade car so everybody can see the President."

March 2004

You know you're a Political Spouse when...

Your telephone repairman/hairdresser's cousin/neighbor's best friend all have some amazing and transformational software for traffic control that he/she wants to sell to the city.

You notice over half the people on your holiday card list are new friends.

You own an African robe, a Chinese embroidered shirt, an Arab kafiya, and a sari—and you wear them all.

You have a dear friend get seriously mad at you about the traffic.

You open a letter addressed to your husband that has cherubic angels around the borders, and you think how sweet until you read that Mrs. Smith thinks your husband should be lynched.

Many people have confessed to you that they're addicted to the Municipal Channel.

A catchy newspaper headline doesn't relate to the story, and you're among the twenty people in the whole city who will notice.

The first thing you do when you get to an event is open the program and count the speeches.

PLEASED TO BE IN THE SHADOW

If I'm at the hair salon or doctor's office, I'm probably enjoying a little Privacy and Solitude. It's hard when someone approaches, calling out, "How's the mayor's wife?" Don't bust me!

April 2004

Pointless Sessions

When Bill was first elected, a local elected official, whom I'll refer to as Greg, called me and said, "I'd like to meet with you. How about coffee at 10 a.m. Monday?"

"Sure," I said without asking the purpose of the meeting. On the morning of the meeting, I drove to the appointed Starbucks and ordered my decaf cappuccino. As I sat down at the table, I was both nervous and excited. For the first time in my life, I felt like a politico. Then as the minutes passed, I became anxious, looking to the door every time someone walked in. Where was he? By the time Greg arrived thirty minutes later, I was annoyed. His first words to me were, "So, why did you want to meet?"

I said, "I didn't set up the meeting, you did."

Greg cleared his throat and recovered. "Oh, of course, I wanted to talk to you about the situation downtown."

I'm sure I just stared blankly at him. He explained, "We need more underground parking."

I had practiced law, then become a stay-at-home mother, and was now a children's book writer. Other than having a parking contract at a downtown garage ten years ago, I knew nothing about the subject. At that moment, I made a promise to myself: I will never assume that just because someone more important than I am asks me to a meeting that he will have something to say.

Jonathan Sandys and me

PURPLE SNAFU

I was getting ready to walk onstage to speak about my book Window Boy *when Jonathan Sandys, Winston Churchill's great-grandson, leaned over to me and whispered in his proper English manner, "Your purple thing is hanging out." I hadn't felt such terror since I was in kindergarten and someone told me that I had a piece of toilet paper on my shoe. I was wearing a green suit. What was purple? And hanging out of where? I frantically patted myself until I spotted a loose shoulder pad that had come untacked and was now flapping around like a kite tail!*

May 2004

Public Speaking

I've always been terrified of public speaking. I'm not shy in conversations with people, just speaking in front of groups. When I am asked to say the prayer in my Sunday School class, my heart starts pounding until it is all I can hear in my head.

A week after Bill was elected, I received a phone call from the United Methodist Women's Association. The lovely woman on the other end of the phone invited me to address a class on the subject of my faith. Just contemplating the invitation, I felt my palms starting to sweat.

I should have seen the handwriting on the wall from the start, but I wasn't ready to face reality. For a P.S., public speaking is inevitable. In the first few months after the election, I turned down the United

Methodist Women's Association and everyone else who asked me to speak.

Not only did I have my fear to contend with, I was certain that I had nothing to say. The person I was before the election certainly didn't have anything to offer an audience. Why in the world would anyone want to hear from her now?

I might have dodged the bullet for a while longer, but a lucky mistake forced me to accept my new role. I agreed to attend an event, but when I received the invitation, I saw myself listed as the keynote speaker!

My fear still joins me at the podium, but since that first speech, I've learned how to ignore my pounding heart. I've learned not to race through a speech to the end so it will be over faster. Oddly, the part of the job that I dreaded the most—public speaking—has given me the most satisfaction. I've learned to almost enjoy it.

A PODIUM SIT-COM!

My friend Annette Strake shared a story about her successful stint as a Political Spouse. When her husband, George, ran for office, she told him, "I'll do everything, but I won't stand behind a podium."

Six weeks later when they were at a hotel for a big political event, her husband said he needed a surrogate.

*In front of the campaign staff, he announced,
"Annette, I have it all set up for you to speak tomorrow.
And they've taken out the podium!"*

*Annette said, "It's the people, not the podium, that
I'm scared of."*

June 2004

Potential Speed Bumps

Political Spouses face a unique challenge. Our personal interests may not dovetail with our spouse's, yet often our spouse's high profile is the only reason we are invited to speak. "Bill thinks…" I've learned this much: speakers who recite secondhand opinions are boring. You have to figure out a way to connect with your topic on a completely personal basis. Once your topic comes from your heart, your speech becomes a great conversation.

Being on the speaker circuit, I also found out the hard way that there is no such thing as "it's no big deal" when you take your place in front of a group.

Before Bill was elected mayor, I agreed to introduce a scientist at an event. Although I asked for the bio beforehand, the organizer told me not to

worry. "I'll get it to you on the day of the event."
As I stepped up to the podium, she handed me the
bio. With no preparation time, I began reading the
bio word for word. Reciting a long list of dates,
honors, and awards, I just couldn't help myself. I
skipped to the final paragraph. Unfortunately, my
off-the-cuff edit omitted a few key facts, and no one,
including me, had any idea why this particular
scientist was at this event.

Dale Carnegie said, "There are always three
speeches for every one you actually give. The one
you practiced, the one you gave, and the one you
wish you gave."

As I hurried to my seat past the confused faces, I
promised myself: I will never force my audience to
endure my lack of preparation again.

P.S. TIP

*Making a speech? Keep it especially short when you are
the only thing standing between the audience and an
open bar. Pass the Scotch!*

July 2004

Prepare for Snafus

To complicate matters in the public speaking arena, I get requests to speak on topics like "How to be positive," "What I wish my mother would have told me," and "How to make good choices." Just think about it: what do you wish your mother had told you? And what part of your answer would you be willing to share with 500 fifth-graders?

I have a good imagination. But when I'm presented with a topic as opposed to having the luxury of choosing one, my mind can go as blank as the computer screen in front of me.

When I get really stumped, I work with a great speechwriter. Ann doesn't write speeches that she would give, but rather speeches that I would give, using my words and reflecting my thoughts. This is essential. It's a collaborative effort from start to finish.

I have fantasized about looking out into the audience of fresh young faces and saying, "You make good choices by thinking before you act." After a quick, "Thank you very much," I'd hurry to my seat.

Even when you're prepared, expect a curveball. I've arrived at events only to find that my audience is all seniors rather than the youthful group that I was expecting. Or that a hundred people are in the audience as opposed to only fifteen. I've thought I would be talking to a group of health care providers and found that I'm actually speaking to their patients. A radical change in the audience alters the content of a speech. After walking into a room and sizing up a crowd, sometimes I've had to face the fact that my carefully prepared speech was worthless. I've also arrived and found a totally different topic listed next to my name on the program. Where did that come from?

Moral of the story: be ready to improvise.

PREFERRED SCENARIO FOR
EVENT MANAGEMENT

Donor names would be listed in the program and never read out loud.

During introductions, the emcee would always ask the audience to hold their applause to the end.

Speakers would sit near the podium and not travel across the ballroom to reach it.

Luncheon events would only last an hour.

Speeches would seldom last more than fifteen minutes.

Rather than a succession of speeches, guests would have some time to talk among themselves.

Speakers would be given a subtle two-minute warning to keep them on schedule.

August 2004

Plan Skillfully

I'm privileged to attend many functions for the great non-profit organizations in my community, and event courtesy is close to my heart. Although charitable events can be fun and enlightening, without careful scheduling, they can become an endurance test of repetitive speeches.

When I'm supposed to speak at an event and the organizer says to me, "We need you to fill twenty minutes," it's a red flag.

What would happen if the organization stopped trying to fill time and instead asked, "What do we want to communicate and how can we best do it?"

Organizers of charitable events are good, enthusiastic people. They know that their event is their only opportunity to convince this particular ballroom full of guests to become involved with their charity. In packing their programs with speeches, the organizers are thinking about how many diapers they could buy for AIDS babies, how many books for children in India, how many trees they could plant. On the other hand, when guests feel that their needs have been ignored, they are less likely to make a commitment to the cause.

Leaving an event, I've heard attendees complain, "We gave our money. They didn't have to torture us, too."

I've also heard people rave, "That was fantastic. I want to learn more."

Often, the difference is simply a matter of time management.

PRETTY SAD

I recently was scheduled for a routine colonoscopy, so I had to keep two days clear on my calendar. It was wonderful. But it's also pitiful when you're looking forward to a colonoscopy in order to have some free time.

September 2004

Precious Seconds

I have always been fascinated by time and its uses. I've even written a book for teenagers about time travel called *Time Cops*. The plot revolves around a conflict between two groups. The Time Designers want to change time to reduce human suffering, and the Time Fundamentalists want to keep time exactly the same.

My bedroom has three large picture windows. I have a chair in the corner with a good light, and I like looking out the window at the pine trees while I write. For whatever reason, a stretch of three or four hours with no commitments is heaven to me.

On the flip side, I value other people's time and hate being late. When I'm tardy and rushing to a meeting, my stomach is clenched; every muscle in my body is tight. To avoid these tortured moments,

I overcompensate. Once when I was due at a luncheon, I had a flat tire on the way. No problem; I had left so early that I still arrived at the luncheon on time.

When you're compulsively punctual like I am and your day includes even minor appointments, you're always checking your watch to see if it's time to leave for the next event. Constant vigilance breaks your concentration and keeps you from ever luxuriating in a stretch of unscheduled time.

To safeguard my time, I try to screen even minor commitments. If I let my guard down, I've found my time splinters into thousands of unsatisfying pieces. With time, the whole is definitely greater than the sum of its parts.

My favorite spot

PROBABLY SCIENCE FICTION?

For one of my children's books, I invented a Preposterous Species known as "time vultures." These characters relentlessly gobble up people's time. For the record, they are totally made up and bear no resemblance to anyone living or dead.

The Reach Out to Dropouts Day walks

October 2004

Persuading Students

My focus has always been improving education. To that end, Bill and I helped start Expectation Graduation, an initiative to keep more kids in school. Every year, on Reach Out to Dropouts Day, volunteers knock on doors and personally ask kids to come back to school. Over 4,000 students have returned to school since our first walk in 2004. A healthy percentage of these students have gone on to graduate.

Imagine this: You're a dropout. It's Saturday morning. Maybe you worked late and then went out and partied with your friends. No teacher has ever come to your home before. A loud knock on the door awakens you. You open the door and find your principal, a teacher or two, your mayor, and other adults whom you don't know standing on your doorstep. Community leaders have come to your home to convey to you a message: you're making a terrible choice. Your mistake will affect not only you but your grandkids.

These young people seem shocked by our visits. No one has ever cared so much before about whether they stayed in school.

I can still picture one young man from last year. He wore the lowest hanging blue jeans I've ever seen. He looked completely bleary-eyed. From our conversations with him, we found out that his mother was in jail and that he was living with his grand-mother. Eventually, we were able to convince him to return to school. He climbed with us into an SUV so we could go back to the school auditorium where he could re-enroll.

Across the street, three grandmothers sat, fanning themselves, keeping vigilant eyes on their neighbor-hood. As we passed, they gave us the thumbs-up sign.

PLEASE SOMEONE ASK SOMETHING

I was at a school talking about my book Window Boy, *and I asked the kids if they had any questions. No hands went up. "I'm not leaving," I told the students. "Not until someone asks me a question." Finally, one little girl raised her hand. "What's the most romantic vacation that the mayor ever took you on?"*

That was an easy one. The answer is "France." Paris was Sensational.

My second book

PAINFULLY SCINTILLATING

FACTS YOU MUST FACE AS A P.S.

PHOTO SHOOTS

PUBLICITY SHY

PERFECT STORM

January 2005

Painfully Scintillating

Prior to Bill's stint as mayor, I was seated next to a man I admired at a dinner party. The food was served late and the time between courses dragged. I tried to hold up my end by talking to my dinner partner about his art collection, his college years, his kids, anything I could think of. For the duration of the lengthy dinner, he never asked me a single question. That wouldn't happen today.

As a Political Spouse, you suddenly get more fascinating—which is a lot of fun! I enjoy and appreciate people's interest. But I try to keep in mind that I need to earn the attention; I don't want to babble on just because I am lucky enough to have an audience too polite to roll their eyes. Occasionally, well-wishers will continue to ask details about my kids' summer schedules, the bridgework I had done, or the time our bathroom flooded long after they could have any real interest. The spotlight is flattering, but I don't want to succumb to the illusion that the details of my small life are fascinating.

In fact, I have to admit that these recollections violate my principles, and I ask the reader's forgiveness. At least I kept it short.

IT'S NEVER A PROPITIOUS SIGN WHEN...

A speaker says, "Your program lists our thirty-eight corporate sponsors, but I would be remiss if I didn't read them to you."

February 2005

Facts you must face as a P.S.:

Your high-maintenance friends will probably
move on.

You'll begin to see some positive aspects of cloning.
Having a few other wives around to pitch in could
come in handy.

You'll want to invent three-year-old triplets. Mothers
of triplets can leave events to go home early.

Despite the fact that your spouse could get a job
making more money and you could enjoy a much
more carefree life, people will tell you with a straight
face, "I hate politicians. They're all in it for
themselves."

Some days, you'll be grateful for term limits, at least for your spouse's office.

June 2005

Photo Shoots

I never have enjoyed having my picture taken. I don't look at photos or cherish them. I prefer being in the present rather than looking back at the past.

When you're a Political Spouse, you're always getting photographed. That's just a part of the deal. I usually don't get impatient; I remember the photographer is doing a job. I try to do mine by smiling in a way that shows who I am. I try to remember how lucky I am to be part of such a great community. When I do this, I find that my smile is more likely to reach my eyes.

In the last few years, cell phones have created more photographers and have increased the number of photographs exponentially. I try to remain grateful that it makes people happy to have a photograph with the mayor.

Despite the fact that I feel as if I am getting photographed constantly, whenever I need a photo for something, I don't seem to have one.

Go figure.

PICTURESQUE SECRET

Lynn Wyatt, a glamorous Houstonian, told me, "Never put your arms around people. It makes you look wide."

As if Lynn Wyatt could ever look wide!

August 2005

Publicity Shy

I grew up with some hard and fast rules that have stuck with me. Don't put ketchup on anything but hamburgers. Never chew gum. And don't have your name in print unless you marry or die. I'd like to think this last rule came from Eleanor Roosevelt's injunction, but more likely the source was a rhyme that was going around when I was a kid. "People's names and people's faces should never appear in public places."

Some people are thrilled when their name is in the newspaper and only get upset if it's misspelled. Others of us grow uncomfortable when our name appears on the printed page. If your gut feeling conflicts with your role as a Political Spouse, it's hard.

However, it didn't take me long to understand how

much charities need publicity. So many people do such good work. How to rise above the noise level and get noticed? Sharing the spotlight can be an effective way to help my favorite causes. In that case, I've learned to welcome it.

Then I began writing books for teenagers. It's hard to sell books; every writer needs all the publicity she can get. So, I carved out two big exceptions to my general rule—so big, in fact, I worry that I've completely lost touch with the original principle. But whenever I think about this, I realize that I don't even know where the original rule came from in the first place.

Besides, I still only eat ketchup on hamburgers, and I never chew gum.

PASS ON STATURE

Some people may try to make you feel more important than everyone else. Once a public figure—or anyone—believes she is more important, her downfall begins.

September 2005

Perfect Storm

When Hurricane Katrina swept through New Orleans on August 29, 2005, the ensuing devastation was enormous. So was the outpouring of love and support from Houstonians.

My memories of those days are still vivid. At the George R. Brown Convention Center, in less than twenty-four hours, volunteers created a virtual city. On Thursday, September 1, at 10 a.m., the convention center was empty. By 6 p.m. that same day, volunteers had set up a command center, two playgrounds, a library, a store of donated goods, and one of the ten best hospitals in Texas. The medical area housed a mobile pharmacy, X-ray unit, and dental center.

At the command center, volunteers from across

the city clustered under handwritten signs that read:
Logistics, Housing, Shelter... Within hours, they
created a virtual organization and began figuring out
ways to make the new residents feel comfortable, safe,
and welcome. Volunteers purchased, prepared, and
served food to an average 6,000 residents a day.

In addition to the incredible competence
demonstrated, it was the loving extras that made
Houston's embrace of the evacuees so special.
A barbershop and beauty salon were staffed by
volunteers. Masseurs massaged tired backs under a
sign that read, "A gift from California."

I have never seen such a fine example of the
volunteer spirit, and I've never been more proud to
be a Houstonian.

A PRAYER TO SHARE

Dear God,

Help me to live in the moment with Peace and Serenity, to celebrate those around me, to always be kind.

Be patient with me because I often get fixed on the goal and forget that life is what happens between goals.

Thank you for the gift of service.

PARTY SENSE

PARTNERSHIP SOLACE

POSTPONE SHAKE

January 2006

Party Sense

Even before Bill was elected to political office, I scrutinized invitations carefully. My personal rule was that once I accepted an invitation, I went unless I was hooked up to an IV. I think Bill and his staff still follow that rule, and they should. People really look forward to the mayor's attending. If he doesn't show up, it's noticeable.

For my part, as I've gotten older, I've begun to cut myself some slack. If a wreck has caused a traffic pileup and the freeway is backed up for miles, if rain is pouring down and the roads are starting to flood, if I have a bad stomachache and am afraid to eat anything, or if I'm running late because the dentist appointment took so long that I will only get to the event for the last five minutes, I don't go. It's unlikely that I'll either contribute much or enjoy it. If anything, my bad day may prove to be a distraction.

When I'm hosting a party, if circumstances stack up in a way that it becomes difficult for one of my guests to attend, I'll say, "Of course, I'll give you a rain check."

I feel liberated since I've begun to shake off my social guilt and accept the reality that my hosts are glad to extend the same consideration to me. After all, we've all experienced days when everything goes wrong. When, despite your good faith intentions, attending a party is just not the right thing to do for you, your family, or your host.

And parties should be fun, right?

POLITICAL SAVAGERY

During the first campaign, our then twelve-year-old son made a very Poignant Statement. He read a direct mail piece prepared by an opponent who was trying to label Bill as a big spending liberal. The mailing had a big yellow duck on the front cover. The piece said, "If it thinks like a duck, quacks like a duck, then it's a duck."

Our son said, "Do adults really read stuff like this?"

March 2006

Partnership Solace

When I was an associate at Locke Liddell, the firm had a five-year partnership track; I didn't make partner the first year I was considered. At that time, I worked sixty-hour weeks and the firm, with its hard-working partners, fast-paced recruiting season, and competent professionalism, was my whole life. The partners at the firm were the people I admired most. My banker clients were some of my best friends. My office with its view of downtown was my haven.

The partnership decision was a blow. Although a few friends stopped by, in a gesture meant to be sweet, someone kept closing my door to give me privacy. The whole side of the thirty-fourth floor felt as silent as a tomb. My colleagues had only the kindest intentions, but for the next few days I felt as if people were avoiding me because they didn't know what to say.

I'm happy to report that I made partner that next year.

Here's the lesson in all of this to me: a kind word and a direct gaze mean the most when you are in the toughest situations. This holds true with public servants and public figures whose hardships are often played out in the public eye. I know it's tough to figure out what to say, but who can misinterpret, "Are you O.K.? You know I'm here if you need to talk. You know I care about you."

I try to send a note or make a phone call, no matter how awkward the situation, because I remember how much I have appreciated the kind words and notes that I've received in good times and bad.

P.S. TIP

Always remember to say, "Good to see you," rather than "Nice to meet you." When I don't remember, invariably I'm greeted with a Polite Snicker and a terse, "I sat next to you last week at dinner!"

November 2006

Postpone Shake

For the past few years, every time one of my kids comes through the front door sick, I catch their illness. Just this year, I've had laryngitis twice and three or four bad colds. Since colds can linger for several days, I generally have to leave my house before they are over.

Which presents the difficult question: Do you go around and shake hands with everyone and become a walking germ factory? Or do you let people know you're sick?

I always let people know that I'm sick. I couldn't act otherwise; I'd feel too dishonest. But this choice sets up a marathon disclosure session. Often, I have to tell a hundred people, "No, I can't hug you; I can't shake your hand; I have a cold."

It's the choice I make, yet I feel like a whiner/ complainer. I feel as if I'm asking for sympathy for a stubbed toe. After all, I have friends on chemotherapy who bravely carry on without talking about it. And it is incredibly repetitive and boring to repeat this message over and over again.

Yet, the alternative is worse. I hate to think of the pounding headaches I'll pass on. The school plays or board meetings that will be missed as my cold spreads. The many sleepless nights my friends will endure as they stay up coughing. So I'm content to repeat my message as often as necessary.

"I'm not going to hug you. I have a cold."

PURELL SECRET!

When you're out and about a lot and you don't want to become a human petri dish, it's a good idea to keep hand sanitizer in your car and purse.

2007

PRACTICALLY SERENDIPITOUS

PRETTY SOCIAL

PERSONAL SELF-DEFENSE

PERSONAL SURVIVAL KIT

September 2007

Practically Serendipitous

In the book I wrote about time travel, *Time Cops*, the time travelers have a word that's a big part of their vocabulary—FLADE. FLADE stands for fate, luck, and destiny. One great thing about being a P.S. is that every once in a while you feel as if you've brushed up against FLADE.

I mentored a young woman, Crystal, a sophomore at Lee High School. Crystal was failing at Lee. I lost touch with her over the summer, and then when I reconnected with her in the fall, I found out that she had "passed high school."

She hadn't re-enrolled in Lee, but she had worked all summer at a grocery store to earn the money for a degree. She paid $300 to an "academy" that was nothing more than a diploma mill.

This is what Crystal told me. "I didn't get a cap and gown, but otherwise my diploma is just the same."

Just the same? She was failing out of public high school and then was able to buy a diploma for $300. Something was wrong with this picture. This particular academy has been operating for over fifteen years in the Houston area.

Now, I'm happy to say that it's under criminal investigation.

PARK SURPRISE

My friend and I walked through a low-hanging cloud at Memorial Park. On the west side, we looked over at the forest buffering the golf course from the track and spotted white parachutes draped in the trees and blanketing the grass. Dissolving Kleenexes? Forest jellyfish? We got closer and found that the mist had lifted up hundreds of spiderwebs. In the center of each, a tiny spider shivered.

No matter how many times I've walked the park, there are always surprises.

October 2007

Pretty Social

A typical evening with Bill: Bill comes home from the office, does his quick change, and we drive over to a school on the west side where he reads a proclamation. Fifteen minutes later, we head to a charitable organization on the other side of town to salute their volunteers. Twenty minutes later, we're on our way to a downtown hotel where he will give a keynote speech on energy policy. I wave at people and shake their hands, but have no time for conversation or connection.

Since my role is strictly one of support, sometimes I don't decide to attend until the end of the day. It takes me thirty minutes to dress if I wash and blow dry my shoulder-length hair. Often, I'll spend a longer time getting ready than I'll actually stay at a single event.

It's tempting to pass on these evenings, but Bill likes me to go with him, and I'm grateful that he enjoys my company. If the organizers aren't expecting me and have no seat at a table for me, I lean against the wall and listen to Bill speak. In those moments, I have to admit I do feel a bit generic.

But I don't mean to complain about being an afterthought. When I think about the alternative— trading places with Bill—the wall is great.

PERHAPS SOMEONE COULD JUST TELL ME WHAT TO WEAR

On invitations, I've seen:

Festive

Smart dinner attire

Casual chic

Casual elegant

Dressy casual

Snappy casual

Country club attire

Festively informal

Fashion forward

Exotic

November 2007

Personal Self-Defense

Because I am a Political Spouse, people contact me about a wide variety of issues. The emails pour in weekly requesting my help on such diverse topics as securing a visitor's visa for an Iranian grandmother, obtaining a new hearing aid for a prisoner in a federal prison, or distributing a new magazine to restaurants around town.

I don't have a clue how to help, but I take the requests as a compliment. If your husband is a leader who gets things done, people peg you for a leader and bring their far-flung problems to you.

Broken traffic lights, faulty drainage culverts, and vacant city lots are within Bill's purview, and I'm happy to listen to people share their neighborhood concerns. But sometimes, acquaintances stop me in the grocery store, health club, or school hallway. During the first few years of Bill's tenure, I dutifully prepared long emails to his office based on these catch-and-run conversations. "You see, the sign for the exit for my house on the freeway is visible when you're going north to south, but not when you're traveling south to north."

Over time, my role as intermediary grew to be exhausting, and I decided that if people wanted my help, they should be willing to make the job a little easier for me. Now, when I get a request, I ask the person to meet me halfway with an email description of the problem and its proposed solution.

I'm not trying to get rid of the request. Call it a test of willingness to accept personal responsibility.

PLAIN AND SIMPLE, I WON'T MISS...

Meetings about the database.

*Giving a delightful party and having everyone ask,
"Is Bill running for something?" "Is a contribution
required?" "Will there be speeches?"*

*The person—his/her face changes—who backs me into
the corner of a room and, despite my protestations, tells
me everything I never wanted to know about…tax
appraisal districts.*

December 2007

Personal Survival Kit

No matter how you shape your role, you will need a few things.

First, a bio. If you give a group your resume to use for your introduction, count on it. They will read it word for word and the audience will snooze. Instead, craft a bio that you can stand to be read aloud. Keep it current.

Eventually, you'll need several bios for different purposes and occasions, but once you have that first one, it's much easier.

Next, a recipe. You'll be surprised how often you're asked for one. Eva, a great cook, gave me a recipe for Buffalo Stew, and we make this Tex-Mex dish on holidays. It's even better on the second day.

Third, people frequently ask about my favorite

My current stack

book. This is a difficult question for me. Asking me to list my favorite book is like asking me to choose a favorite child.

I much prefer the question: What are you reading now? I always have an answer to that. I just finished *Lone Survivor* by Marcus Luttrell and *Three Cups of Tea* by Greg Mortenson and David Oliver Relin.

Both great books.

PREPARING BUFFALO STEW

2 tablespoons olive oil
1 large onion (chopped)
3 garlic cloves (minced)
1 pound mushrooms (sliced)
1 teaspoon oregano
1 teaspoon cumin
1 1/2 pounds tomatillos
1 cup chicken broth
1 bunch cilantro (coarsely chopped)
2 pounds ground turkey
1 (15 oz.) can white hominy
1 cup corn (frozen)
Salt and pepper to taste

Heat 2 tablespoons oil. Sauté onions for 10 minutes.
Add garlic, cook 4 more minutes. Add mushrooms
and spices. Boil tomatillos for 5 minutes in chicken
broth, and then add cilantro. Brown the meat in batches
and mix with onions and mushrooms. Cook for a
minute, add tomatillos and hominy, and simmer for 30
minutes. Add the corn and simmer another 15 minutes.
Season with salt and pepper to taste.

SERVES 6-8

2008

POLITICALLY SAVVY

PRESSING SITUATIONS

PRIVATE STUFF

SERIOUSLY, YOU KNOW YOU ARE A
P.S. WHEN... PART II

PLANTED SECURELY

January 2008

Politically Savvy

When I talk to schoolchildren about writing projects,
I explain to them that great ideas don't come with
fireworks. They can be little more than a picture,
a half thought, a glimpse of an idea. It's the writer's
responsibility to develop the idea, believe in it, grow it.

One aspect of public life is that people come to you
with ideas. We're working with a group now to
blanket Houston with bluebonnets. How wonderful
would that be? Sometimes, people want your help
turning the idea into brick and mortar. Often, they
would like for you or your spouse to take the idea and
bring it to fruition.

An idea is like an oil rig in an untapped territory.
Many steps are necessary to take an idea from its
inception to full-fledged production. There is no

assurance that the idea—even if it's a great one—will be a producing well, not a dry hole.

Good public servants are interested in results. Bill and his staff are busy working on basic services. In most cases, a political team (or couple) just doesn't have the resources to adopt even a marvelous idea and breathe life into it.

I am a believer that the world would be a better place if schoolchildren—and everyone else—accepted the challenge of turning their own great ideas into reality.

PULPIT SCARE!

We were at a church sitting in the pews and I heard my name called. Without warning, the minister said, "Now, Miss Andrea White is going to come up to the pulpit and lead us in her favorite church song."

As I was walking up the aisle, the only song I could think of was Happy Birthday.

January 2008

Pressing Situations

Public servants spend their days trying to help other people. Their overscheduled lifestyle is exhausting, and one of the facts of political life is that families need to find days and ways to care for the caretaker. Listening, sympathizing, or just showing some special attention can help.

Bill really likes to bicycle, and occasionally he'll take a long ride in the country. Being outside is one way that he relaxes. He needs to find ways to replenish himself.

A problem can arise when another family member says to him, "O.K. Now it's my turn." I really have no response when my husband says, "I can't come home now. I'm expecting a call from the President."

This particular line isn't one that I've heard

often, but I've heard many equivalents. Long ago, we stopped waiting for Bill to eat dinner. He was too often delayed at the office. I would grow angry while our spaghetti and green peas grew cold. I stay in a better humor if I just eat when I get hungry.

So how do I make peace with this? I think that if I had access to all the information that Bill does and knew about all the people he was helping, I'd make the same choices with his time that he makes. On good days, I succeed in remembering.

PLUS SIDE OF POLITICAL LIFE

Bill's job brings me in contact with some real heroes, some of the greatest volunteers in the world. It is an honor to be around the people who have started day care centers, homeless shelters, and community centers, people who make a real difference. It is also incredible to be part of such an intelligent team as the people who work for Bill and support us every day with their cheer, good sense, civic responsibility, and mindfulness.

July 2008

Private Stuff

We've all been riveted by breaking news accounts of politicians who cheat on their spouses or are caught in some sting operation. Just like reading fiction, watching the lives of public figures gives us the opportunity to put ourselves in an unfamiliar situation, test our own character, and ask ourselves, What would we do?

I think this thought process is legitimate and fair. But I feel sickened when I hear criticisms of wives standing by their husbands at press conferences. It may not make sense to us, but we don't know all the pressures these families are facing. What if one or more of their children might be fragile or vulnerable?

As a mother, I understand the need to do the best you can for your family. Your number one priority is to end the media show as soon as you can. How can you end it? By acting in a way that kills the story. If you don't stand next to your husband, that's another story. If you do, it's a story, but a smaller one.

I try to be slow to judge other people and to take into account what they should not have to share.

POLLS AND SURVEYS

You can conduct your own informal polls by questioning cab drivers. I often ask them what they think of our mayor. One cabbie looked in his rearview mirror and met my eye. He said, "Our mayor is color blind. He treats all people the same." His response made me a Proud Spouse.

August 2008

Seriously, you know you are a P.S. when... Part II

You've been humbled by the kindness of Perfect Strangers too often to count.

You've been to a firefighter's funeral and seen the fire ladders leading up to the sky.

You feel at home in many houses of worship.

You've cried at many funerals for people you never met but who have given their lives in public service.

You realize what a small segment of the city you've lived in all your life and actually know.

You've dragged yourself to an event and come home feeling energized by the encouraging words and unexpected warmth of others.

POLITICAL STATEMENT

Republicans and Democrats who are active in the political process have more in common with each other than they do with people who are unengaged.

September 2008

Planted Securely

When I think about what a Political Spouse should be, I visualize a belayer in mountain climbing. In climbing, belaying is the technique of controlling the rope so that a falling climber does not fall very far. The climber, your spouse, is on a steep cliff and has a rope tied around his waist. You are on the cliff over-looking the rocky face with your feet firmly planted on the ground and are holding the other end of the rope.

The belayer becomes the climber's eyes and ears on the ground. From your vantage point, you have a better view of the side of the mountain and can tell him which way to turn for the best path downwards.

Although it is tempting to want to climb down and help, it is important to resist that urge.

If the climber stumbles or falls, as long as you

have hold of the rope, he will survive.

I feel as if I can be more useful staying grounded.

POSITIVE SIGN

A First Lady Fact: Grace Coolidge, the wife of Calvin Coolidge, was instructed not to talk to the media. Pressed into Silence, she obeyed by responding in sign language!

Conclusion

Please Share

Most of us have our hands full living our lives, and only occasionally do we find the time to jot down our memories. These notes are all I have down on paper to remember the years of my life during which my husband served as Houston's mayor.

I offer this slim volume as encouragement to each of you: Please Sit down and do a better job than I did of writing your own story. Then, if you're willing, Please Share some of your Precious Stories with me at Andrea@passionatesupporter.com. I'm especially interested in stories about support roles.

What happens when a loved one accepts a responsibility that requires more time than any single person is able to give? Do you and your loved one approach everything as a team? Or do you try to set

some boundaries? Has your support of your spouse,
relative, or friend led you to your own passion?

I'd love to hear—and learn—from all you
Passionate Supporters out there.

A Note about the Author

Andrea White is an attorney, author, education activist, good friend, mother of three, almost lifelong Texan, and the First Lady of Houston. After graduating Phi Beta Kappa from the University of Texas, she attended the University of Texas Law School and went on to become one of the first female partners at the firm now known as Locke Lord Bissell and Liddell. She has published three books for teens: *Surviving Antarctica, Window Boy,* and *Radiant Girl.*

BOOK DESIGN

HILL
Houston, Texas

COVER PHOTOGRAPHY

Terry Vine Photography
Houston, Texas

PROJECT MANAGER

Roni Atnipp

PHOTOGRAPHY CREDITS

Kim Bonner
Page 11

Franci Crane
Page 68

Cindy Fitch
Page 103

Quyen Le
Pages 8, 22, 25, 32, 34, 38, 53, 57, 70, 97, 107 and 114

Janice Ruben
Page 48 (Digging Photo)

Lorelei Rao
Page 86 (Cots Photo)

Adrian F. Van Dellen
Page 16

DEDICATED TO

Franci Crane, Joe Jamail,
Nancy Kinder, Dr. Maconda O'Connor,
and Edi, Robin, and Bonnie Reed,
each of whom deserves a chapter in this book

THANKS TO

Scott Atlas, Roni Atnipp, Jenny Bailey,
Brené Brown, Gail Brown, Gracie Cavnar,
Lucy Chambers, Susan Cooley,
Ann and Kenny Friedman, Chris Hill,
Sis Johnson, Quyen Le, Karen Otazo,
Julie Pippert, Pam Rosenauer,
Susan Santangelo, Ellen Susman,
Bobby Van Lenten, Lorraine Wulfe,
and Michael Zilkha

SPECIAL THANKS TO

Ann Boor

blurb.com